HOW POLITICS FAILS US
What We Should Know About
Our System Of Government

Table Of Contents

Introduction

Definition of politics: *Ideology where real world consequences and truth take a back seat to personal prejudices and compromise.*

I suppose politics has always been a dirty game, played by those with power to gain and little substance to offer their constituents. It's not that they don't have the skill set to provide positive guidance and civic improvements for the rest of us. It's more likely that they lack the incentive to fight the system that they become ensconced in. After all, it provides them with a level of benefits that you and I could only hope for. Short of running for reelection, there is so little work to do, and being productive in the law-making process is not a target.

Samuel Clements, writer & humorist: *"Imagine that you are an idiot. Then imagine that you are a member of Congress... wait, I repeat myself"*

Participation in government has been structured to provide a degree of luxury and job security far beyond that which is deserved by the participants. A self-serving seniority system has been developed that allows those who take up the top rungs of the ladder to exercise enormous control over those who are situated below them. Equality among Congresspersons is merely a figment of the imagination of those who are without a clue. As a result of this structure, little gets done that does not play into the quest for power by those at the top.

I suppose it is natural that being in the 'public service' with all of its heady perks would give any ordinary person a terrific ego boost. The problem, however, arises when one's ego becomes larger than one's brain. Invariably what we end up with, much like that which occurs some business environments, are candidates who are mostly being voted into their level of incompetence.

Plato, philosopher: *"One of the penalties for refusing to participate in politics is that you end up being governed by your inferiors."*

So do I feel that government is essentially corrupt and without any redeeming value? Not Completely. If the politicians were thoroughly worthless, this country would not occupy the position that it holds on the world's stage. It is just that they could do better… as a matter of fact, considerably better. But then that would require raking over the coals the power system that makes them so very comfortable and so very unresponsive to the people's interests. It would mean giving up the easy reelection money with the incumbent obligations that come from the loose purse-strings of big business. Fat chance.

It has been said that politicians are interested in four 'P' things - Power, Perks, Pork and the polite version, Privates.

From My Perspective

My definition of politics: *Ideology where real world consequences and truth take a back seat to personal prejudices and corruption.*

I suppose politics has always been a dirty game, played by those with power to gain and little substance to offer their constituents. It's not that they don't have the skill set to provide positive guidance and civic improvements for the rest of us. It's more likely that they lack the incentive to fight the system that they become ensconced in. After all, it provides them with a level of benefits that you and I could only hope for. Short of running for reelection, there is so little work to do, and being productive in the law-making process is not an ambition.

Samuel Clements, writer & humorist: *"Imagine that you are an idiot. Then imagine that you are a member of Congress… wait, I repeat myself"*

Participation in government has been structured to provide a degree of luxury and job security far beyond that which is deserved by the participants. A corrupt, self-serving, seniority system has been developed that allows those who take up the top rungs of the ladder to exercise enormous control over those who are situated below them. Equality among Congresspersons is merely a figment of the imagination of those who are without a clue. As a result of this structure, little gets done that does not play into the quest for power by those at the top.

I suppose it is natural that being in the public service with all of its heady perks would give any ordinary person a terrific ego boost. The problem, however, arises when one's ego becomes larger than one's brain. Invariably what we end up with, much like that which occurs some business environments, are candidates who are mostly being voted into their level of incompetence.

Plato, philosopher: *"One of the penalties for refusing to participate in politics is that you end up being governed by your inferiors."*

So do I feel that government is essentially corrupt and without any redeeming value? Not Completely. If the politicians were thoroughly worthless, this country would not occupy the position that it holds on the world's stage. It is just that they could do better... as a matter of fact, immensely better. But then that would require raking over the coals the power system that makes them so very comfortable and so very unresponsive to the people's interests. It would mean giving up the easy reelection money with the incumbent obligations that come from the loose purse-strings of big business. Fat chance.

It has been said that politicians are interested in the four P things - Power, Perks, Pork, and (the polite version) Privates.

The 2-Party System

'System' is an appropriate descriptor for the manner in which politics is pursued in America. It permits candidates to start with a roughly fifty-fifty chance of being elected to office, which is not too bad for persons who have few qualifications beyond oratory. After that the system takes over. And unless they seriously screw up once they are in office, they are in like Flynn.

The logic that for some justifies our outmoded electoral process may be that a time and money-consuming, three-party, run-off is not required. The person with the most votes is not forced to negotiate a platform with multiple parties, as is the case with other countries.

A downside to this method of selection is that party platforms become inflexible since money flows to those platform positions that are of interest to big business. In other words, party positions become rigid to avert an interruption in their campaign financing. The result is that important issues may have little chance of receiving or surviving a fair hearing.

So what is this fixation that voters have with party affiliations anyway? Am I missing something important here? Is one side mostly mistaken with their particular platform while the other side is mostly correct with theirs? Is it the herd instinct in play?

Friedrich Nietzsche, philosopher: *"Insanity in individuals is rare - but in groups, parties, nations, and epochs it is the rule."*

To top off this unrealistic must-go-with-a-party mind frame, some states require voters to sign a party-designated registration prior to voting. Then there is the ill conceived but foolishly convenient option of voting a straight party ticket, which only perpetuates the its-my-party silliness. Why should people vote for a gaggle of candidates that they are not familiar with on poorly thought out philosophical grounds? Why should we believe in a black and white political world when life is cast in shades of grey? How did we become to be so myopically one-sided in the first place? Well perhaps it is the herd instinct.

Mark Russell, humorist: *"You've got the brain-washed, that's the Democrats, and the brain-dead, that's the Republicans!"*

Bill O'Riley of Fox News said surprisingly to his credit during the 2008 campaign that he did not care much about the individual parties. He just wanted to know the politician's positions on the issues. I can just hear some witless voter saying *"But you can't have positions without having parties"*.

Unfortunately both sides in the political game are, as usual, short on specifics and long on pandering platitudes and disingenuous sound bites. Getting away with this self-serving, anti-voter-interest conduct can be partially attributed to people's lack of ability to assess what is being told to them. If one is continually being deceived by irrelevant arguments, who is at fault…those who are the liars or those who allow themselves to be lied to?

George Orwell, author: *"In a time of universal deceit, telling the truth is a revolutionary act."*

I was at a luncheon when one of my friends pulled out a local absentee ballot and asked others at the table if they knew some of the people on the ballot. One attendee wondered if this ballot was for just one of the parties. The answer was *Yes*. Apparently my friend had no fondness for anyone from the other party or their platforms.

Shouldn't we consider that both parties have a few decent ideas to offer and more than a few ideas to reproach? So why is it that so many of us are adamant about supporting a single party of their choice? I can account for a few possibilities in support of this peculiar behavior. It may be that people...
-- became interested in a particular party as children when their acceptance level was high - *a form of indoctrination*
-- grew up in an environment *(rich or poor)* and related to those interests and the party that was most intimately linked to their pocketbook - *a form of it's all about me*
-- became involved with a party that was popular with their social group or their campus mates - *a form of follow the leader*
-- they researched the differences between all of the candidates and made informed judgments - *a rare form of intelligence*

What are the chances that the last possibility is the one that leads to most people's party affiliation? Slim to none I expect. If even a small amount of due diligence were involved in approaching party-choice decisions it would be impossible to align one's self with a single party on all issues. Being an independent that decides matters on their merits makes more sense. But then we do not always use this logic and common sense as our guide to forming opinions. Mostly we are persuaded by influences *(good and bad)* that we encounter around us and find enticing.

James Bovard, Civil Libertarian: *"Democracy must be something more than two wolves and a sheep voting on what to have for dinner."*

On the positive side, in 2011 it was reported that 40% of us now consider themselves to be Independents. This is a far cry from the 10% of just a few decades ago when only loony bins were so inclined. It shows a significant disaffection with the polarization that has been shamelessly demonstrated by both parties.

In 2012 the satisfaction level with federal politicians was reported to be a measly 9 percent. The decades of political nonsense may finally be coming home to roost, but I wouldn't hold my breath. I suspect it will be many years before the politicians truly get the message from a mostly silent electorate.

On the Larry King show in 2010, Jesse Ventura, ex-professional wrestler and ex-governor of Minnesota, suggested that the main problem with the politics is that we are "subjected to the Republicans and the Democrats". He went on to say that their staged antipathy toward each other is accounted for by two things. They…
-- are phony, like professional wrestling *(politicians _do_ socialize in private)*
-- act against the best interests of the country *(by putting their own interests first)*

John Adams, President*: "In my many years I have come to a conclusion that _one_ useless man is a shame, _two_ is a law firm and _three_ or more is a congress."*

Mother of Deception

There are beliefs that can be beneficial, and there are those that work against our welfare. One of the more counterproductive ideas is that our country is being governed by the politicians for the benefit of their constituents. Even a cursory examination of their political behaviors and lack of effective governing should make these failures evident to all but the most indoctrinated or disinterested.

The reality is that our political leadership has long since given up their autonomy to the interests of major corporations and their collection of lobbyists with deep pockets. How these politicians vote on any issue has been subjugated to a desire to be reelected to office. This means accepting whatever campaign funding that they can lay their hands on, regardless of the attached strings. Knowing this fact about politics, corporations willingly subsidize the reelection efforts with contributions to both parties, while at the same time exacting a toll of loyalty. Could their making political payments to both sides be any more telling about their motives?

Political decisions, policies, and laws are not being made based on concerns for the interests of the public. If that were the case we would not be...
-- the last industrialized country without an decent healthcare system
-- encouraged to buy massive SUVs and trucks for routine use
-- traveling to Canada or Mexico to purchase drugs and healthcare at reduced prices
-- constantly being misled by a flood of false advertising, which now occupies about one third of television viewing time thanks to deregulation years ago *(early regulations permitted stations to have only six minutes of commercials per hour)*
-- wondering why there is so much cancer, while at the same time eating contaminated foods and permitting corporations to pollute the environment
-- thinking about the cost of school lunches rather than being concerned with their nutritional content
-- spending billions on wars in countries that are not worth saving because it suits our military-industrial-complex
-- having our citizen's interests systematically subverted to those of big oil, big drugs, big banks, big insurance, etc.

Does anyone think a $40 billion profit in one year by Exxon is even remotely reasonable? That is more than $100 for every man, woman and child living in America, or about $400 per average family that is bestowed on just one of the big oil interests.

Becoming a Lobbyist

Going back to lobbyists for a bit, just who are these people anyway, and how can they exercise power over the political process. Well I am not aware of any college offering a course or degree in this profession. That means that the skill has to be learned on the job. I am also not aware that there are openings advertised in the want ads for such wannabe candidates. What that means is that these people have to be self-promoted into the occupation.

Ok, how does that fortuitous situation come about? It starts by their getting to know people in positions of power. And what better way is there than to be a sitting member of Congress or a high placed staff member of such a person. In addition to one's official duties, learning who is who and who is not becomes a valuable trade. And *trade* is an appropriate descriptor since being successful in this field requires the ability and resources to do horse trading. Quite often that means trading perks for votes.

Lobbyists, contrary to the opinion of the uninformed, do not go before Congress just to present a companies viewpoint. Their job is to promote that viewpoint by what ever means may be at their disposal. As a rule that task involves applying whatever pressure they can bring to bear to help Congresspersons see the light.

So congress, in an effort to be all things to all people *(except for the voters)*, goes along with the flow which can push them up-stream toward reelection. And when it is their turn to retire from office, there are ready jobs for many of the politicians, staffers, and department heads who found it future-convenient to cooperate with business's who sought out their favors. And not so surprisingly, they are offered those jobs that sometimes involve becoming a lobbyist or executives. So lobbyists, Congresspersons, and corporate executives have a nice round-robin club going for themselves.

Changing Landscapes

When I was younger, the makeup of political parties ran along liberal and conservative fiscal lines. The questions were...
-- who paid for what - federal or state
-- who had the authority - federal or state
-- how much legislation should be directed toward or against business
-- how much welfare would be doled out to the needy
-- how much social security should be returned to the retired
-- how much power should unions hold
-- how big or small should government be
-- what industries should we subsidize, if any
-- do we bail out large companies that get in trouble
-- do we balance the federal budget

The Republican Party was generally known to be on the side of smaller government and bigger business, while rarely throwing a bone to the poor. The Democratic Party was in favor of tossing money at problems rather than coming up with real solutions. Since those happy days...

-- both parties have joined the race to see how much spending they can get away with because it suits their reelection efforts
-- Bill Clinton, for example, took as many issues away from the Republicans as he could - regardless of his actual political heritage or beliefs
-- Carl Rove did the same for Bush by accusing the Democrats of the same issues that were Republican's weak suits
-- political pork projects have gotten even more out of control - like the multi-million dollar bridge to nowhere in Alaska just to make Senator Ted Stevens look good to his constituents - which was subsequently cancelled by then Governor Palin, who then kept the funds in Alaska anyway.

In Recent years a change of political behavior became very clear. Republicans, having been hurt by their minority status, decided that just say "no" was more than an anti-drug philosophy. It became their marching song.

Another of their platforms has been the promotion of religious dogma by conservatives who can't seem to mind their own business. When Jack Kennedy, a Catholic, ran for President, he promised that religion would not influence his political judgments. When George Romney, a Mormon, ran for President he made essentially the same pledge. Their religious preferences were a private matter and were not up for consideration as public policy.

Today the advocates for religion have once again come out of the closet, predominately filling the ranks of the Republican Party. They work to inflict their views on legislation at all levels of government. I suspect that resorting to a theocracy (God based government) would be the culmination of their dreams. Just look how well that has worked out for the Muslims.

The problem with merging church and state in government is the intolerance factor. Faith-based advocates are generally not the live-

and-let-live types with a gentle agenda. They would happily put the force of law behind their rigid mindsets, and move the rest of us into lockstep with their obsessive need to promote religious concepts.

Making abortions illegal would presumably be high on their targets of opportunity. Even if that particular issue is of no consequence to you, there could be other dictates to impinge on your rights and freedoms. And to what good end, if any? The world has never been well served when religion controlled the helm of a government.

As for the intolerance issue, perhaps minding one's own business would not be a bad starting point, as opposed to the relentless march toward a *follow-the-leader* mentality. No one has a lock on right and wrong, and no one should be allowed to promote their religious focus through the force of law.

To be fair and balanced politically, the Democrats have their share of radicals among their ranks as well. The main difference is that they seem to be more people-problems-to-excess oriented rather than their counterpart's business-profits-to-excess oriented. Being people oriented is directed towards getting votes. Being business oriented is directed towards re-election funding.

Regardless, this does not excuse either side from any extreme viewpoint. We need to reject extremism and instill tolerance, conciliation, and compromise as the appropriate model for problem resolution and social advancement. The only alternative to this is a continuing, unnecessary, state of contrived strife among politicians with little legislative progress to show for it.

In recent elections the Democrats have come up with a devious plan for retaining office. They buy votes. Illegal you say? Perhaps so technically, but not in reality. Why do you think so little has been done to keep out the poor from the Americas to the south? They tend to vote Democratic in support of the dole that is bestowed on them. If you do not see this as buying votes, you have my sympathy for your higher taxes that result.

In 2014 a poll showed that Congress had only a 9 percent approval rating. That's more than nine out of ten who feel that they are not doing a good job. So one has to wonder how these politicians are immune enough from negative public opinion to continue unfettered with their do-nothing agenda. Well the answer that I have come up with is that their quest for power blinds them to certain realities. And the heard instinct tells them that all is well… if so-and-so can do it and get away with it so can I.

For and Against

As we should all know by know, politicians are consistently against virtually all proposals that are proffered by their opponents. The ugly sport that they play is to bash their adversaries, while at the same time offering little of worth in exchange. This occurs because if one is on record as being in favor of specific ideas they might have more difficulty selling their votes to the lobbyists.

An even darker view of politics is that public display of disagreement on issues is a game of let's pretend which is designed for the public's consumption. It is a manufactured derision that consists of posturing and obstruction. Votes are sometimes taken in the open, but the issues may be decided in the so-called, smoke-filled, back rooms. More often then not it is the most powerful members of Congress and their corporate backers that hold an undeniable sway over the less powerful members.

Does anyone remember when it was that compromise became a four-letter word in government?

The prevailing attitude in congress is that politics is essentially about confrontation and not about compromise. Perhaps newly elected legislators do expect to use negotiation upon arrival in office, but very quickly they learn that the boss-controlled system is alive and well in Washington. This is the protected environment where those who are at the top of the party ladder dictate their party's voting policy to those members who are on the rungs below them. They are able to accomplish this task because they control advancements, perks, and appointments which lead to…
-- being recognized to present bills
-- being given better office accommodations
-- advancing to more prestigious job positions

-- going on travel assignments
-- receiving additional pay

The impetus of the senior politicians is to appease the lobbyists and to badmouth the opponents. *Give nothing and propose nothing* has become the political battle cry. As a result we have a smokescreen of exaggerated animosity accompanied by very little productivity in Congress. This behavior is shameful beyond words, but few of us are willing to acknowledgement it and demand a change. The natural result of Congress's failure to consider other's points of view is that vital issues may be sidelined or diluted.

In 2011 and 2012 Congress reached its zenith with the squabbling over a budget limit, spending, and taxes. This propensity to avoid these real matters is infamous in government, but somehow that behavior does not lead to embarrassment because so few of us are objecting to the sideshow.

When he was first elected to office, Governor Schwarzenegger of California failed miserably with initiatives that were directed at changing, as he saw it, the state's outdated policies. This occurred due to his aggressively going up against the entrenched powers, and his doing little to consult with the opposition. It was simply a matter of the terminator in action. But Arnold was a person who could learn a lesson from failure. Eventually he set up a smoking tent where both parties could get together to work out their differences… and with some success. What a novel idea to turn your opposition into your confederate.

Since politics is primarily the business of getting reelected to office, that means defeating one's opponents by any method at one's disposal, using fair play or not. While a responsible voting record should be sufficient to produce these same results for an incumbent, the truth is that voters have virtually no idea what the representatives in their jurisdiction actually stand for or vote for beyond a few sound bites. Some may know what a politician's public pronouncements are, but this is a far cry from their being privy to politician's actions and intentions.

When was the last time you saw a politician's voting record in print? Rarely? Maybe never? Why isn't this information offered to us by the press on a regular basis? On one occasion I read an article about a Governor's complete veto record, which was presented as a measure of her mindset. I was impressed with the details that were presented in print. But this rare reporting was the exception that proves the rule.

Problems With Power

One of the problems with elected officials is that they have developed a system where the longer one is in office, the more power they may accrue for themselves over other members with lesser tenure. To put that into perspective, all Congresspersons are not treated equally when they take their seat of office. For junior legislators, the concept of one-person one-vote is actually one-person no-real-vote. Those have long since been sold to the highest bidder or put under the thumb of the members above them.

This also means that the Congressional leadership is the major recipient of corporate funding in order to have them promote the corporate interest and policies down through the ranks. In a very public statement in 2011, the Senate Speaker told his conservative colleges to fall in line on a particular fiscal issue or risk losing their plum committee assignment. Enough said? Well actually not...how dare he!

A possible solution to this corruption of values would be to set term limits for politicians into law. No congressperson could then serve more than two consecutive terms. To be fair to those who are members of the House of Representative would have their two year terms extended to six years, like the Senator's terms. Should various congresspersons be particularly well liked, they could run again after an absence from office.

This change would accomplish several things...
-- no congressperson would have more than one incredibly wasteful reelection campaign
-- politics would be more inclined toward public service rather than providing themselves with a job haven

-- lobbyists would have less incentive to dole money out to congresspersons for their loyalty because they might actually become independent *(lame duck)* politicians if reelected
-- the need to cultivate lobbyists would be so abated that the congresspersons might actually vote on the citizens behalf
-- the powers of congressional leadership would be drastically diminished by virtue of shortened terms and diluted seniority
-- it is likely that the cast system, with committee heads holding much of the power, would come to an end

Jesse Ventura, ex-governor of Minnesota: *"Politics is the worst business in America."*

An acquaintance of mine had an opportunity to travel with a member of Congress on a fact finding mission, and was stunned to see what a thirst for power that person had...
-- kiss-up assistants were at his beck and call
-- no request for frivolous service would be turned down
-- he ate at the best restaurants, with food and drink prices meaning nothing because they were paid for by the public
-- special favors were expected and given wherever he went

So is it any wonder that these representatives sell their votes so easily to stay in office? Their attitude of entitlement also rubs off on the President and his wife. It has been reported that while First Ladies generally had two or three assistants. Michelle is said to retain in the neighborhood of twenty. Dare we say there are visions of royalty dancing through her arrogant head? And of course there are the frequent, personal trips that the President and his family take at the taxpayer's expense. So much for his caring who pays for a round of golf at about $1.000.000 a pop.

Edmond Burke, writer: *"The greater the power, the more dangerous the abuse."*

Privilege for the Privileged

When a small-engine plane crashes there may be 1 or 2 investigators normally assigned to look into the case. But this was not the normal situation when the pilot happened to be the son of US Senator Inhofe.

The National Transportation Safety Board (NTSB) assigned 7 from the NTSB, 3 from the FAA, and 4 from the plane's various parts manufacturers to study the details of the crash. Anything to try to show that it was not pilot error, which is overwhelmingly the normal case in small plane accidents.

They also interviewed some 20 others consisting of flight controllers, a flight instructor, and the widow who was asked to detail his eating, sleeping, drinking, and snoring habits. And the money required to pursue this operation was apparently not an object of consideration.

A private plane crash might warrant, under some circumstances, as many as 5 investigators to be involved, but this was not the case with John F. Kennedy Jr. He rated 45. Other celebrities and politicians have also scored higher than normal with the scrutiny their crashes. I suspect that there may have been substantial pressure brought to bear in those cases as well.

Speaking of Speaking

It is interesting to note <u>when</u> it is that a politician is outraged enough to make an issue of something. It predominantly occurs when they are defending their misbehaviors or are seeking reelection to office in a tight race. The insiders in Washington are of course privy to why this pompous rhetoric takes place. So Congresspersons apply the appropriate grain of salt to what is being said, even when they are being made a target.

They also know that their fellow politicians do not ordinarily go out on a limb because they have much to lose. They...
-- must first run their ideas past the powers that be, or risk censure if they step outside of the party line *(Just look at the Republican pinhead in 2010 that defended BP, and quickly offered the lame apology that he was misunderstood. He had been confronted by the leadership and told to retract his statement or step down from a prized committee post)*
-- can lose precious bargaining chips that can be bartered with other politicians or lobbyists
-- might risk alienating some of their constituents by being candid
-- can not easily deny what they say in public

Remember the line from The Godfather or the advice that Jackie Kennedy-Onassis ostensibly received from her mother? It went something like: *Never tell anyone what you are thinking so they can't use it to your disadvantage.* For this and other reasons, politicians rarely express their innermost thoughts unless they are desperately in need of publicity for their home campaigns, committee posts, and when a degree of honesty would benefit them.

Sound Bite Politics

With the advent of huge campaign war chests and frequent access to TV broadcast time, politicians have long since discovered that their seconds-long ads work well for them. This politicking technique succeeds because a message can be delivered to the public without the opportunity for return information *(criticism)*. As a result, these nearly valueless sound bites are not challenged as they might be in a debate or community forum.

The consequence of this format is that…
-- there is a lack of pertinent information disseminated because image creation, not content, is on the agenda
-- opponents are painted with false or negative ads that serve no educational reality, but they may stick in voters minds when they go to the polls
-- issues and platforms are typically ignored in an effort to avoid offending anyone, with platitudes ruling the day
-- the press contents itself with news about $400 haircuts, slip-of-the-tongues, and other issues because they are in business of <u>creating</u> sensationalism for a scandal-thirsty public

The sound bite politics employed today have several implications in that they…
-- show a shameful disrespect for the voter by not delivering real information
-- isolate politicians from experiencing or having to responding to contradictory points of view
-- permit politicians to imagine that they have an understanding of new bills - which they don't since they may not even read the laws that they vote on

-- turn politics into show business

Wrong Side - Again

In 2015 it had been reported in the news that there was a mini-movement, once again, to have restaurants and (especially) fast food chains label the nutritional values of their food... and not just the calorie counts. Apparently there are more women and Democrats In support of this issue than there are Republicans, whose mantra has long been: business is self regulating and government should stay out of business. Sure they are. While the Republicans do not have a monopoly on bad judgment, too much political posturing on the part of both parties is supported by the unrestrained corporate bribes at the expense of consumers.

No Where to Turn

Those of us who have an interest in in-depth information about our government's apparatus may be relegated to receiving their political analysis *(he says humorously)* from comedians like Bill Maher and John Stewart. The problem with this venue is that their guests are predominantly liberal, and they may not have balanced presentations. Don't conservatives have something constructive to say, or even a sense of humor? If you watch people like Hannity of Fox News, humor and fairness can be as ethereal as a light breeze. He's a liberal basher in the extreme, which involves the repetitive voicing of mean-spirited innuendos and falsehoods.

The problem associated with many of the media's talking heads is that they anchor news programs which are populated with biased reporters and guest propagandist who...
-- may have no solutions
-- might show no insightfulness
-- espouse mostly anti-opponent-party lines

When they happen to book opposing point-of-view spokespersons at the same time, the airwaves are filled with...
-- annoying childish banter
-- irrelevant arguments

-- frequently interrupted statements

All of this verbal nonsense may leave voters with the accurate feeling that there is no one listening to them, and that they might have no better choice than to give up on the system. Not so surprisingly this realistic attitude works to the advantage of the incumbent politicians. They are then free to carry out their re-election efforts with minimal scrutiny from voters.

Bill Maher, comedian: *"Freedom isn't free. It shouldn't be a bragging point that Oh, I don't get involved in politics, as if that makes someone cleaner. No, that makes you derelict of duty in a republic. Liars and panderers in government would have a much harder time of it if so many people didn't insist on their right to remain ignorant and blindly agreeable."*

When there is the occasional criticism from the press, news editorials, or public protest, it rolls off politicians like the proverbial water off a duck's back. They clearly have more important business to focus on, which may not involve listening to their constituents. So much for having an effective representative-democracy in this country. While the Constitution framers wrote in fairly effective checks and balances on the three branches of government, someone apparently forgot about addressing the non-performance of elected officials. I guess they assumed all would take care of itself.

Coffee or Tea Anyone

In 2009 and 2010 we saw the temporary creation of the ultra-liberal Coffee party and emergence of the ultra-conservative Tea party. The latter came into being as a reaction to two situations... a lack of effective political leadership and the frenzy that was whipped up by the polarizing talking-heads. They gave people the impression that they were not being listened to and that Congressional spending was heading the country toward bankruptcy *(we should all recall the downgrading of the US's credit rating in the past).*

While there may-have-been/may-be something positive to say in regard to both parties' platforms respectively, people have not gotten the idea that voting an incumbent out of office is more effective than blowing off a lot of hot air at town meetings. What better method do we have to send a message to ineffectual Congresspersons than to remove them from office?

Vote for the opponent - the incumbent has already become corrupted.

In the 2014 election, in spite of Congress having an even lower regard by the voters than the in-the-toilet rating of Obama, the electorate chose to bring back many of the incumbents to office. Apparently their feeling is that the lack of substantive progress by Congress was caused by the other guy's candidates... it was they who were the bums, not my guys/gals. This vision demonstrates how little people actually know about what their candidates are up to and what part they are responsible for in the political failures.

Holy Clinton-ism

On The Daily Show, Bill Clinton was a guest in 2008. He suggested that politicians have a really tough job, and that this is why they may be beholding to Political Action Committees *(PACs)*. If you buy this self-serving drivel, apparently politicians have to spend most of their time flying from Washington to their home states in order to raise campaign funds, to the point of exhaustion. Well, who developed that alleged system anyway? You? Me? Hardly! It was the incumbent politicians who wanted to maintain an edge over their rivals so that they could remain in office without having to resort to merit, even though they know that the current system is corrupt and legislatively ineffective. Should we really feel sorry for them?

If politicians wanted to correct the election process they have the power to make if happen. After all they make the laws, don't they? The reality is that reelection to office is far more important to them then is their public service. Bill's whimpering about their difficulties is nothing short of a pathetic vehicle used for creating a diversion, one which attempts to shield the politicians from their irresponsibility. My guess is that he made these statements because he did not want to be tainted by the negative truth about campaigning, or its exposure to the sleeping public.

The Election Process

Many years ago I was asked to give a speech on any topic for a sales training course. After giving some thought to a subject matter that might not be in the mainstream, I elected to argue the merits for and against voting. It was at that point that I realized that I might not vote again. Needless to say, virtually no one in the class agreed with me on my do-not-vote side of the equation.

In spite of being repeatedly told by politicians that every vote counts, the reality is that every vote is worth (*ta da*) exactly one tiny vote, or virtually nothing. The pundits and politicians love to point out the one or two small town elections that were decided by a single or handful of votes as proof of their thesis.

The reason that we are constantly fed this propaganda is because it is a deliberate effort to prevent people from realizing how powerless they actually are on their couches. It does not take a mathematician to recognize that one vote out of ten million equals exactly one ten-millionth of the total number, a really miniscule fraction. When the people are told and therefore believe that they are effective in controlling the political process, then those who are actually in control can reside comfortably, unrecognized in the ether.

From another perspective, in some cases your vote may actually turn out to be worth nothing, no matter who it is cast for. It's called Super Delegate. This is where the party faithful assign themselves to a delegate status without ever being voted in by the citizens. With the Democratic Party *(isn't that a misnomer)*, one fifth of the delegates to their recent conventions were these unelected good-ol boys and girls. They can cast their vote for any candidate that they choose, and they are responsible only to themselves. They are free to make backroom deals with whomever they choose, for their own benefit if desired.

Short of the unlikely potential of public opinion having some power over super-delegate voting, we have no controls levied upon them. Perhaps the most disturbing aspect is that when asked, these same people will defend this system in spite of its glaring injustice. This is why your one ten-millionth of the total vote may be worth zero. I assume that you appreciate standing in a long line to vote, right?

When I watch the Presidential election process *(especially)*, there is one inescapable conclusion that comes to mind. The real power brokers must be amused at the pointless, non-issues-raising talk that constitutes the debates, speeches, and sound bites that are made by the candidates and their surrogates. Don't those who watch these charades know the difference substance and pontificating? Don't they actually know that government doesn't work, and why that is? Is there a minutia of consciousness among the voters as to who is actually running the country and what they are up to behind the scenes? The answer to all of the above questions is No!

When we don't pay attention we deserve the results that we receive. Good government is not an accident. Rather it is the result of people having knowledge and concern about its activity. The net result is that big business runs America in the background, and they do not much care who happens to get into office. They must be pleased that their control of process is seldom revealed or is obscured by those doing their bidding.

In 2008 the Democrats took control of Congress and then what? Virtually nothing changed from when the Republicans had the power. There is just more of the same old bickering to cover up the fact that all of the politicians are beholden to the same interests that throw money at both parties. And that the politicians share the same obligations to provide these businesses with their service. Could it really be any other way with our morally and ethically corrupt two-party system?

Why do you think there is so much inertia against...
-- third party candidates
-- government negotiated drug prices
-- reasonable term limits
-- a simplified tax system

Why do you think there is so much legislation that is skewed in favor of...
-- investors and business - laughingly justified by the unproven trickle-down theory

-- tax incentives for big oil, while they make billions of dollars in excessive profits
-- loopholes for the rich that most people will never know about, much less be able to use
-- subsidies that were originally designed to benefit mom and pop farms but now are mainly used to support corporate agribusiness
…and the beat goes on.

Owning Your Mistakes

There is something a little bit dysfunctional in our nature that induces us to unnecessarily cover up failures, shortcomings, and mistakes… especially for politicians. Because the press can occasionally be ruthless in its quest for sensationalism *(as opposed to news)* this may be an almost understandable practice. No one wants to be put in the awkward position of having to defend a reasonable past behavior by responding to the slanted interrogations of the sensation seekers. It takes valuable time and detracts from more important issues, if there were any. Even a lie will stick if it is given enough air time. But this fact of political life does nothing to justify the wide-spread deceit and corruption that is prevalent in our elected officials.

John Kennedy took an unusual action for a politician some time ago by taking the blame for the military's Bay of Pigs fiasco in Cuba while President, even though he though it could have been attributed to a CIA intelligence failure. His mea culpa garnered him respect and contributed to a boost in his popularity. On the other hand, Richard Nixon denied his guilt in the Watergate cover-up for as long as he could, and was consequently pressured into resigning in disgrace. A personality defect caused him to preferred lying to revealing his and his associates flawed and felonious judgment.

John Fitzgerald Kennedy, President: *"An error doesn't become a mistake until you refuse to correct it."*

A press-created issue a few years back involved an attack on the waterboarding of captured terrorists. In 2013 Rudi Giuliani, in a discussion regarding drone attacks, said the George Bush would not have gotten away with Obama's drone policy, as witnessed by the flack over water waterboarding. My take on this is that it only became an issue because of the administration's cover-up, not necessarily the appropriateness of the interrogation technique. Politicians don't get that lying changes everything.

In 2011 when Congresswoman Giffords was shot in Tucson, the press was quick to blame the vitriolic politicians and their own talking heads for their violence-inciting rhetoric. While I am inclined to support a degree of that logic, they went off the charts in singling out Sarah Palin *(no fan of mine)* for using gun-sight cross-hairs on her target map of the candidates that she wanted to be defeated in the 2010 elections. Then to compound matters, her staff claimed that these icons were surveyor crosshairs. Now Sarah is a woman who lives with guns and not surveying equipment. So rather than copping to a rather innocent use of this icon, she and her staff chose to fabricate a less than believable explanation. I guess being branded a liar by some is just part of doing business as usual.

People are generally forgiving of mistakes when the offender owns up to their gaffe and expresses contrition. When they don't, that's another matter. For politicians, the first line of defense often appears to be lying. If they had even half a brain they would know that there are no secrets for any length of time. Perhaps they rely on the public loosing interest in whatever the issue was that they lied about.

While I'm referring to guns, the right wing took the position *(once again)* that guns don't kill people... people do. This of course flies in the face of the strong correlation between too many guns and too many shootings.

In the case of Giffords, a congressman suggested that there was no merit to limiting gun clips to ten rounds to prevent a similar carnage. He said that he would be able change to a new clip in mere seconds. This lightweight thinker conveniently ignored the fact that Gifford's shooter was tackled while trying to load another clip in his weapon.

In 2014 a similar event occurred in a public school. A hall guard tackled a shooter while he was trying to reload after shooting three students. Why can't we make the simple connection between the free flow of guns into the hands of almost anyone going hand and hand with their increasingly-frequent and deadly use?

The Distraction Factor

Because Congress and the administration are all members of the same exclusive club, they will depart only so far from being silent in order to berate a fellow colleague. Yes, they rant on over petty issues about the other party to the ears of the voters, but they do not often engage in personal or meaningful attacks against their opponents except during elections when their job survival is at stake. This restraint is a bipartisan effort at political self-preservation.

In a 2008 hearing, the head of the Justice Department was exposed for giving false testimony to a Congressional committee, which is a felony. So did he lie? Apparently not! Did he go to jail? Not that either! Then when a same-party politician was asked to comment on the situation, instead of offering an honest opinion he responded that the person had been "inaccurate", which amounts to a lie about a lie.

Political credo: If I don't reveal your shortcomings, you may not expose mine.

Kip's Books & Links

The books listed here are available in ebook format for Kindle™ and Nook™ readers at Amazon.com and elsewhere. Some of the shorter materials are "ideas" booklets or excerpts from longer books. Hard copy books are available at Createspace.com. The URL links, where listed, access book previews.

A BETTER BATHROOM - An Ideas Guide
Construction
https://www.createspace.com/Preview/1134187
$1.99   34 pages

A BETTER KITCHEN - An Ideas Guide
Construction
https://www.createspace.com/Preview/1134190
$1.99   36 pages

AGGRESSION & BULLYING - It's Not Just Our Wiring
Human Nature
$1.49   11 pages

AN OUTDOOR KITCHEN - The Latest Trend?
Construction
$1.49   6 pages

BEFORE STARTING HOME CONSTRUCTION - What You Need To Know In Advance
Construction
https://www.createspace.com/Preview/4136208
$2.99/$5.49   40 pages

BRAIN CHOICES & FREE WILL - Getting To Know Ourselves Using Concepts That Are Not Well Understood Or Accepted
Human Nature
https://www.createspace.com/Preview/1134191
$3.99/$5.99   78 pages

CUSTOM HOME DOs & DON'Ts - The ULTIMATE Guide To Getting Your Custom Home DONE RIGHT!
Construction
https://www.createspace.com/Preview/1134192
$6.99/10.49   266 pages

DECEPTION IN AMERICA - How We Are Manipulated Big Business, Politicians, The Press & Our Indoctrinations
Government/Business/Politics

https://www.createspace.com/Preview/1134195
$9.99/15.99   458 pages

EVOLUTION, THE BRAIN, & RELIGION - How Evolution Made Us What We Are
Human Nature
https://www.createspace.com/Preview/1134196
$4.99/$6.99   160 pages

EXCESSIVE EXECUTIVE COMPENSATION - What You Should Know About
The Fleecing Of America By Executives & Boards
Government/Business/Politics
$1.49   11 pages

FOLLOWING THE CROWD - How We Fall In Line With Others
Human Nature
$1.49   14 pages

FUN WITH APPETIZERS - For Those Who Like To Entertain Well
Cookbook
https://www.createspace.com/Preview/4438108
$3.99/$5.99   70 pages

FUN WITH CARBOS - The Cookbook For Those Without A Care
Cookbook
https://www.createspace.com/Preview/4440041
$3.99/$5.99   94 pages

FUN WITH CHICKEN - The Fowl & Seafood Cookbook That Avoids Red Meat
Cookbook
https://www.createspace.com/Preview/4441007
$4.99/$6.99   148 pages

FUN WITH DESSERTS - The - What To Do When The
Meal Is Over - Cookbook
Cookbook
https://www.createspace.com/Preview/4444531
$2.99/$5,49   64 pages

FUN WITH ENTREES - Getting To The Heart Of Cooking
Cookbook
https://www.createspace.com/Preview/1135491
$5.99/$8.99   172 pages

FUN WITH MEAT - The Carnivore's Cookbook
Cookbook
https://www.createspace.com/Preview/4436803

$3.99/$5.99   110 pages

FUN WITH SALADS - My Take On The Classics & Others
https://www.createspace.com/Preview/1136150
$1.99/$5.49   24 pages

FUN WITH SEAFOOD – See Food & Eat It Cookbook
Cookbook
https://www.createspace.com/Preview/4494327
$3.99/$5.99   84 pages

FUN WITH SOUP - It's Economical, & Healthy As Well
Cookbook
https://www.createspace.com/Preview/4442511
$1.99/$5.49   38 pages

FUN WITH WINE - Aging And Tasting Wine
$1.49   9 pages
An informative guide, including wine-term explanations.

GOVERNMENT FOR PEOPLE? - How the US government "functions" without regard for the negative ramifications of its actions
Government/Business/Politics
https://www.createspace.com/Preview/1134204
$3.99/$5.99   88 pages

HOME DESIGN GOALS - Important Considerations
Construction
https://www.createspace.com/Preview/1134209
$1.99/$5.49   36 pages

HOME GREEN HOME - The Ins & Outs Of Home Efficiency
Construction
https://www.createspace.com/Preview/1134208
$2.99/$5.49   42 pages

HOW BUSINESS FAILS US - What You Need To Know About Business Corruption
Government/Business/Politics
https://www.createspace.com/Preview/1134206
$2.99/$5.49   70 pages

HOW WE LEARN, WHY WE DON'T - Getting To Know Ourselves
https://www.createspace.com/Preview/1134212
$3.99/$5.99   86 pages

INCONVENIENT REALITY - How Big Business Shoots Us In The Foot, & How Congress And The Press Helped Get Us Into This Mess
https://www.createspace.com/Preview/1134213
Government/Business/Politics
$5.99/$8.99   190 pages

INVADING YOUR PRIVACY - What You Don't Know And What You Should Know
Government/Business/Politics
$1.49   18 pages

LAW IS FOR LAWYERS - The People That We Rely On For Our Protection Can Be The Biggest Offenders Of It
Government/Business/Politics
$1.99   22 pages

ONE POT CLASSICS - The Comfort Food & Easy Clean-up Cookbook
Cookbook
https://www.createspace.com/Preview/1134289
$6.99/$11.49   306 pages

PATHETIC POLITICS & PERFORMANCE - What We Should Know About Our System Of Government
Government/Business/Politics
https://www.createspace.com/Preview/1134290
$4.99/6.99   112 pages

POWER BREEDS ABUSE - Or To Put This Another Way… On Some Level, Power Always Leads To Corruption
Government/Business/Politics
https://www.createspace.com/Preview/1134291
$2.99/4.99   48pages

SELECTING A CONTRACTOR - Making The Right Choice The First Time
Construction
$1.49   11 pages

SELLING & STAGING A HOME - Getting The Most From Your Efforts
Construction
$1.49   6 pages

SENIOR FRIENDLY HOME DESIGN - Making A House Safe
Construction
$1.49   11 pages

SOCIAL NETWORKING - The Downside To Exposing Yourself

Human Nature
$1.49   5 pages

THE PRESS'S ROLE IN BAD POLITICS - What They Do, And How They
Contribute
Government/Business/Politics
https://www.createspace.com/Preview/1134295
$1.99/$5.49   32 pages

THE WAR ON DRUGS - How It Harms Everyone
Government/Business/Politics
$1.49   6 pages

TO SELL OR REMODEL - Making The Right Decision
Construction
$1.99   9 pages

TRAVEL DEALS & BARGINS – Gaming The System To Win
Travel
$1.49   14pages